Getting old?
Well, maybe just a little!

Other books by Harlan Carl Scheffler

Alzheimer's: Observations & Disclosures & Resolutions (George Ronald)
The Challenge: Teaching the Children
The Quest: Helping Our Children Find Meaning and Purpose (George Ronald)

Getting old?
Well, maybe just a little!
&
The Myth of Mortality

by
Harlan Carl Scheffler

illustrated by
Harlan Carl Schefflet

George Ronald
Oxford

George Ronald, *Publisher*
Oxford
www.grbooks.com

*A catalogue record for this book is available
from the British Library*

ISBN 978–0–85398–584–6

Cover Design: Steiner Graphics

Contents

Publisher's Note   vii
Introduction   ix

Part One: Getting old? Well, maybe just a little   1
Part Two: The Myth of Mortality   19

Author's Note   57
Bibliography   59
References   61

Publisher's Note

Harlan Carl Scheffler signed the contract for the publication of this book on 30 March 2014. On 7 April he passed away, before he could see his book published. We at George Ronald, Publisher, are honored to have worked with him over a number of years and pay tribute to his life of service.

Introduction

Throughout our formative years thoughts of getting older were put aside; there was too much growing up to do to be bothered with such matters. Even if we had taken the time to think about it, we couldn't have pictured ourselves old and wrinkled, sitting quietly on some front veranda, watching the world pass by. However, no matter how young we might be, each new day draws us closer to that sleepy porch setting with its rocking chair waiting. I recall a down-home incident that unaccountably left its mark in my memory. Through some now forgotten circumstance I found occasion to drive past the old people's home in Batavia, Illinois. This was back in the mid-forties. The red brick block-shaped two-story structure looked institutional, somehow foreboding. A massive, ominous metal-tube fire escape was attached to an upper floor window slanting precariously to the ground; in an emergency the old folks could be dropped down the chute. A lone figure was sitting on the porch. As I drove past, I caught a glimpse of his hand waving. I had a fleeting thought: *'Hmm. I wonder who lives in such a place as that.'*

Well now, my own days have rolled by, one after the other, a great number of them, and the months have turned into years, actually more than ninety, so I feel I know that old fellow; I think I know him quite well. This I know for sure: he and his quiet surroundings are very good friends. And who is he? Well, he is not just anybody. He is a father, or grandfather, maybe a brother or uncle; someone who can no longer take care of himself. In this regard he could be anybody, though actually he looks very much like me. Watch as he glances up and waves; listen carefully; his voice is sort of wispy, like mine . . . what's he saying? I can't quite make it out. 'It's me! It's me! I'm in here! It's me!' Gracious; that's ridiculous, surely he cannot be me! No? Well, read on.

Residences for old folks – condominiums, retirement communities, assisted care facilities and nursing homes – are ready and waiting for all of us – if we live long enough. After keeping our noses to the grindstone, there comes the day when we will look up, squint a bit, glance around to see that we are finished working at full tilt and now it is time to slow down; let the next generation take over. Actually, a life's cycle doesn't take very long. After our growing season is completed and the withering and waning begin, it becomes obvious; it's time to take a deep breath, rock back and forth a bit and watch the new generation kick in. Hmm . . . can't be sure, but it seems to be picking up speed; yup, it's in a hurry for sure.

For some reason we have been taught that the coming into existence is a happy time and the process of bowing out is a dark phenomenon to be postponed by any means possible. Let's live to be a 110! The whole proposition would be more reasonable if we could look at the coming and the going as neutral – both just necessary to the operation of life's cycle. Albeit, we seem to be obsessed with the ebbing process, loading up on pills and enduring procedures which essentially do little more than give back to the coffers all our worldly goods which, we must reluctantly admit, is cyclic itself. Keeping old folks alive is expensive. I could dig up some astronomical figure representing the cost of our health care. After our life's savings are used up, the cost of caring for us falls heavily on the immediate family or on the larger community. Suffice to say it appears we want to prolong this life for as long as possible, no matter what the emotional and/or monetary costs might be. Reverting to earlier alternatives seems unlikely; old folks a generation or two ago were cared for in the home, but this is no longer practical. And there are tales of earlier times, stories of Native Americans and Inuits who, at the end of their lives, would find a patch in the forest or hunker down on an icy plane and patiently wait. Apparently the fear factor was overcome by a 'radiant acquiescence', a willing compliance with the natural order, where everything contributes its share until that share is used up.

However, today, as we approach the end of our earthly life, the learned fear of an unknowable future looms menacingly. Our starting out was welcomed with great jubilance, although there were no assurances of any kind. Could it be we became fearful because of what we were taught throughout our growing-up years? We were promised that if we behaved ourselves a commendable reward would be waiting. If we somehow did not measure up – bad news! The impact of this simple lesson stayed with us throughout our lives; the equation popped up everywhere. It was one of our first lessons: *If you misbehave, you will get a scolding* (when I was little the threat was a spanking). *If you are "good", you will be rewarded with a smile and a pat on the head.*' Then, later, when we were too old to spank, the threat became serious: a slow roasting over Hell's fire took over. Mercy!

Be that as it may, part of being human is the 'burden' of having a conscience wherewith we weigh the lessons of right and wrong. With the awareness of the moral, or ethical, aspects of our conduct we are constantly assaying propositions that come our way. Secretly we are ashamed of a selfish act and when we do something 'good' we take a private bow or curtsey. Nonetheless, when old age closes in and it appears our time is running out, we cannot be sure if the Ledger shows that our good column has enough entries in it. Were we good enough to get the ultimate pat on the head? Hmm. Best prolong things. The threat and promise of that blazing pit are so terrifying we will do anything to preserve and extend our life spans, oftentimes far beyond their practical limitations.

However, getting old is such a gradual process it is hardly noticed – until we are blowing out another candle on the cake. Although illness or accident can drastically speed up the process, today you and I are unaccountably privileged to be living our lives at this time when science and its applications are often able to rearrange dysfunctional systems, to correct the abnormal behavior of our atoms and molecules so as to resume their normal congruity. Many failing systems are able to respond to such remedial measures to the end that the world will still have the pleasure of our company . . . even though we may hardly have breath enough to blow out all those candles.

*

This essay is in two parts. The first section is an introduction to the main theme. It is a verbal sketch of the interim between our productive years and the winding down and 'conclusion' that will follow. Although much has been written about the aging process, geriatrics being a rather new science, the reason this essay might be of particular interest is because it is a documentary written by one who is actually experiencing the process of dying, not an outside observer. What is happening to us as we face idle times and experience the need for special and determinate care? Overall, this is an interesting and important inquiry because it has been a neglected topic that we have put aside, tainted perhaps because of its unpleasing prospective. However, this interval time can be most rewarding, for it allows us to review our own lives, to scan through the pages of our Ledger and see how we fared. It is a time to learn what others have experienced through their span of years and it can be most enjoyable and enlightening to family and friends. It is revealed that people are wonderfully diverse, the one attribute that unites us all!

The second section of this essay examines the evidence for life's immortality; it is treated as the natural adjunct, the extension and expansion of the initial phase of our lives, not the end. It is a fascinating subject. Surprisingly, employing the light shed by today's technologies we are assured that death truly is impossible.

Part One

Getting old? Well, maybe just a little

Well, here I am sitting in my rocking chair, watching the world pass by. It is a restful setting, comfortable. I was led to this assisted care facility by way of my wife's illness and now I am alone but not really lonely. These are quiet days, so I have lots of time to paint watercolors and write and reminisce. Without any real schedule, my days mosey along but strangely the weeks and months fly by. I am 92 years old and have several health issues that need special care: my kidneys and lungs and spleen and gizzard are OK but my heart is about worn out. I am one of 120 residents living in this facility. My one-room apartment is quite adequate. With the aid of a walker to keep me steady, I count 86 steps three times a day to the dining room. Every morning I have two fried eggs, over easy, toast burned perfectly, orange juice and coffee. I sit at table 34 with two Bobs and a George. Our dining room is very pleasant; flowers on the table; napkins folded intricately. How strange that I should be so favored. This was not so prevalent a generation ago.

*

My father was one of those who were not the beneficiaries of today's modern medicine or professional care. Fifty years ago he suffered a stroke. Hurriedly responding to a phone call from my mother, I arrived at the house to see my father in the living room lying crookedly on the couch. The doctor was there and the ambulance was on the way. Dad could not move or speak. He was taken to the hospital and, after his prognosis was determined, he was sent to a local nursing home. It was an unpleasing, white-frame two-story structure, a former residence built perhaps a few years after the turn of the century. If I remember correctly, it needed a coat of paint. My father was a man of distinction and this most unbecoming residence and the inept care he received were abhorrent. He was incarcerated, secluded alone in a darkened upstairs bedroom. There was not one occasion when I went to see him that he was not soiled, his private parts raw. His 'nurse' called him 'dearie'. You might ask why I permitted this to happen; I have asked myself this question many times. The only reason I can think of is that I acquiesced to the doctor's judgment; this facility was on his list. I knew nothing of nursing homes. Back then, just 50 years ago, such facilities were mostly not very nice places.

*

One of the more remarkable consequences of living our lives during this particular time is the benefaction that scientific investigation and its applications have brought us. The Industrial Revolution of the 19th century moved the production of things from the home to the factory and soon to follow was the flowering of scientific discovery, particularly knowledge gleaned through medical research. This intellectual blossoming was portentous. So many frailties that accompany the process of aging have become the subject of inquiry. Thus, in the span of a generation or two, many longstanding disabilities have been identified and often remedied through the instrumentation of scientific research and treatment. The study of aging is covered by the term 'gerontology': the inquiry that explores the physical, mental and social changes in people as they age. The researchers who examine the aging process are called biogerontologists. Geriatrics, a more familiar word, is the study of health issues that accompany getting old. During the past 50 years much has happened in these fields and in those that are contingent; for certain, specialized residencies for the elderly have become commonplace. And these assisted care facilities are certainly not forbidding: they are quite elegant, functionally designed to be finishing schools for the aged. But how do we tell our loved ones that they are no longer able to care for themselves, that it is time to move out of the house, give up driving the car and tending the garden and forfeiting decisions; what day is the right day to broach the subject and how do we start? It is a heavy weight. We are asking them to leave behind all the attachments they ever knew; time to take up residence in one of these facilities like, say, Winding Trails at Sunnybrook Meadows.

'Oh my, this is just beautiful. Look at the garden and, oh, the flowers. Mom, remember your garden out by the garage? Let's go in and look around, maybe have lunch. We don't need to make any decisions yet; we're just looking. Oh my! Mom, see over here; they have a video room and, oh, look at the beautiful fish tank. Remember our tropical fish, the guppies and angel fish? I think you would like it here. You'll have your own room and make new friends and Jim and I will be, you know, real close – just at the other end of the phone. Oh, look over here; there's a library. Look at all the books. Look at all the books.'

As nice as these places are, there is a pall that hovers over them; it is not their shroud but ours. Our perception of aging veils the reality and normality of getting old: 'I may not be as quick and strong as I used to be, but I'm certainly not ready to be locked away in one of these awful places! I can get along quite well at home, thank you!!!' Little children, our great, grand, kids dance through these halls laughing and jumping. They have not yet learned. They are too young. When they become teenagers, they will start to understand less:

'Hey, kids! Get ready. We have to get going. Yes, we know its Sunday, but its Aunt Martha's 90th birthday, remember? Did you finish her cards? What? What? Well hurry, get them and come on, let's go. Where's the cake? Oh, ok; and the present; who's got the present – and the flowers? Ok, ok, here we go.

'Settle down; we're almost there. Remember, when you go into the room give Aunt Martha a hug and wish her a happy birthday. Kids! Come on now, this isn't funny, shape up. We won't be there long.

(Whispered) 'Which room is it? Hmm . . . 1402, over this way. Ah, here it is.'

(Extra loud and too fast) 'Hello Aunt Martha. Did we waken

you? Happy birthday! We've brought you some flowers and a cake. (Kids!! Give Aunt Martha a hug!) How have you been Aunt Martha? Is everything going ok? We haven't been doing much, just going along. Marcy's going to graduate in June and Bobby still has two more years. (Kids! Put the games down; give Aunt Martha your cards.) Is your back still bothering you? What's the doctor say? Hmm. Yes, I suppose it will take a while. Oh . . . Aunt Martha, we thought you might like to share the cake with some of your friends . . . Have you met any new ones? No? Hmm. Well, I suppose it takes a while. Oh gosh, look at the time. We have another stop to make, Aunt Martha, so we had best get going. We're running a little late. We'll see you soon. Happy birthday, Aunt Martha, happy birthday.'

(Hushed) *'Whew! Come on, let's get out of here!'*

Am I exaggerating? Perhaps. But there is an onus, a tribulation that is set deep in our consciousness that puts aging and all that is implied in a negative light. It would be better if young children were taught the realities, which sooner rather than later they themselves will be facing. And, more than that: the young and the old would be together, together spiritually, not separate and apart and dysfunctional. The family would remain intact. And even more than that: young people would gradually learn to see beyond 'appearances'. And why is this important? It is important because meaningful things are 'within'. When taught differently, children will become insightful. They will then see the reality and not let outward appearances distract them. It is a simple matter of awareness. The children will learn to observe and to think and to question, and they will become keen and bright with understanding.

(A friend's slightly pertinent story) Grandma had come for a visit; it was Ellie's third birthday. One morning while grandma was showering, Ellie had to use the bathroom. A knock on the door and the announcement of Ellie's plight apparently did not override the sound of the shower so when grandma pulled back the bath curtain and saw Ellie she was taken aback. But her surprise could not match little Ellie's, who, looking up with mouth and eyes wide open, sputtered, *'Grandma! What happened?'* Being three, Ellie couldn't imagine that wrinkled cheeks were not only on either side of grandma's nose.

Accepting the fading of life as positively as we welcome its blossoming will depend on the kind of education we give our children. How they see life is a learned perspective. Today grandma and Aunt Martha are no longer in the back bedroom. They are more often in one of these retirement centers. They are out-paced by today's bustling world. Assisted living implies care, and this is what old folks need. We need to be cared for at the end of our cycle – just like we were at its beginning.

Assistance in living is not something that we call on just when we get old. One way or another we are in need of others to help us find our way throughout our lives. Not one of us makes this journey alone. Parents selflessly provide guidance for their children. Wives and husbands support and encourage and sacrifice for each other. Where would we be without the nurturing of caring teachers who help us learn, particularly to differentiate between knowledge and understanding? Could we get by without the doctor or the farmer or grocer? Lawyers and artists and scientists? We are dependent on others constantly. What about friends?

*

Well, the above is preliminary to the purpose of this essay. I thought it important to describe what I have found to be a common yet a hidden attitude towards aging, held by those who are still caught up in the world of fleeting opportunity and responsibility. I have been a resident in three assisted living facilities for almost five years. Hence I thought it would be interesting – even perhaps helpful – if I could share my thoughts about what it's like 'living in a place like this'. The glossy brochures tell their side but what about the residents' side? Before entering this new environment, I had no idea what might be waiting. What should I be concerned about? I was still the outsider envisioning the old fellow seated in the rocking chair – up to the moment when my dear wife Barbara and I entered this new environment. We moved from a rural setting in southern Indiana. Our log cabin home, pioneer-like, was nestled in the northern hills of the Smokey Mountains range. This was our place of retirement for 20 years. Then, some eight years ago, Barbara was taken downward with Alzheimer's disease. As the symptoms progressed, we and our children decided that it was time to avail ourselves of the care that an assisted living community could provide. In making such a move, we had to filter through everything that we had accumulated over 56 years of being together. In a very real sense we were being called upon to embark on an uncharted journey, a trip that is not considered normal in the flow of life's circumstances.

During our working years, Barbara and I had put aside enough funds to retire. We had not lived extravagantly and this simple regimen allowed us to hold the deed to our cabin property and, with the benefits of Social Security and the distributions from my Independent Retirement Account, we figured we would be able to get along. However, we had not prepared for the cost of assisted care and, after recalculating, we speculated that we could finance our needs for perhaps only three or four years. We would have been well advised to consider critical care insurance early in our marriage to offset this later financial drain. Nor had we prepared for the drain on our emotional resources. Because of the stigma that is still attached to nursing homes, the fear factor suddenly confronted us. *Are we actually going to end up in one of these places? Are we going to be sitting in rocking chairs waving to people who chance to pass by?* It was frightening and confusing. When your cycle is wearing down, stepping into the unknown is most daunting. Decisions! We need help with decisions.

However, once the decision is made, the fear begins to fade away. You are busy with packing and then unpacking, putting things in boxes, musing a bit to reassess their value, and then taking them out. *This is going to Cheery Charity; and this? Hmm – I think Sally would like this for her children when they get a little older.* Clearing away the mental cobwebs, you begin to sense more clearly what is important and what is not. In our particular situation, because of Barbara's illness, everything took its place behind the primary concern for her safety and care. It was relatively easy to classify what was important and necessary and what was not. Actually, when you face up to things, look at them squarely, it is surprising how little you really need. Many of the 'trappings' you have accumulated do not really matter all that much. Getting rid of things is actually refreshing.

So, lightening the load is a good thing, a plus. As the moving date approaches you are surprisingly, increasingly, aware that you have already moved on. You are no longer approaching the bridge but you are crossing it. Your friends look on, mystified by your acquiescence. They hardly know what to say. You look up and smile.

Now the cabin begins to look less like home. Its warmth and charm were not infused in its logs and stone hearth. When we finally close the door, it will be just a cabin in the woods. Barbara and I will take its life with us; we and our children and our friends made it a home. Now it is just a log house waiting to be born again.

So, things are looking better. As I close and mark another box, thoughts hopscotch. I list things we won't have to be concerned with anymore. We will no longer need to shop for groceries and cook and iron (occasionally) or mend, patch, paint, wash, wipe, scrape, scrub, polish, mow, plunge, dust, mop, sweep, rake or clean the cat's litter box (oops, I still have to do this), and, well, et cetera, et cetera. It occurred to me that, when you own a home, one way or another, you have to mindfully regard everything. Nothing escapes: walls, floors, ceilings, large and small furnishings, even yards and gardens and fences and driveways and roofs and shrubs and trees. Everything requires attention. Whew! Things are indeed looking better.

Well, finally! Here we are; we have arrived! Now what? Well, there are questions that should be asked. We want to be certain that the pictures in the brochure do not distract us, that the smiles on the faces represent real smiles. I was a commercial artist in the advertising business for 50 years, making drawings of people, places and things, so I am apt to be cautious. Every time I left the art director's office with an assignment under my arm, the last words I heard were, '. . . *Oh, and Harlan, make it look good. You know, "dress it up a bit".* ' The last five words really meant make it look better than it really was: shinier, longer, bigger, rounder, tastier, grander, smoother, more smiley – more appealing than the truth. It is a harmless ploy? '*. . . certainly we wouldn't intentionally deceive people; that wouldn't be fair; deep down they really know what it's all about.* ' But assisted living brochures' smiles do catch our eye. Perhaps TV sets the pace. Every commercial shows everybody smiling. Even dogs and cats must be screened to measure up to a prescribed degree of glee; otherwise, back to the pound. The TV host's welcoming smile is constant, mask-like, replaced with a momentary look of despair when the news is bad, but that happy smile quickly returns with the next teleprompt. Are all those smiles and happy faces covering up something, something hollow? And what happened to the young newscaster or weatherperson? Where did she go? On her 35th birthday did she suddenly become inept or was it just a wrinkle that the cosmetologist couldn't cover up?

When we get out the old family album that our grandmother put together with such care, the black and white photographs describe, as candidly as is possible, what was going on. Grandma standing alongside grandpa seated was an honest portrayal. No empty smiles. What we are looking at is an example of truth hidden behind appearances. Were they gleefully jubilant? Most likely not, for life was not easy. Even though their countenances are impassive, we must assume they were content, certainly persevering, for they were together for many years. No cover-up.

So, commonplace smiles are suspect. Genuine smiles are soul stirring. Ambling through a shopping mall some time ago, I happened upon a cute, curly-haired two-year-old tot sitting in his stroller. His parents were close by. He looked up at me, stretched his little legs and smile-giggled. He can have no idea how I treasure his gift.

We can put aside the physical surroundings. Today all these places are attractive with their ponds and gardens and trails. What we are looking for is a residence that will accommodate the life we bring to it. Without residents, it is just an elaborate building; without residents the staff would have no reason to show up for work. We old folks hold much power in our trembling hands.

√ *The First Necessity: Put the facility on the defensive. You are in control. You will be paying your share of every salary, meatball and paperclip.*

Taking care of elderly people who have special needs requires not only well-trained employees but a staff of people who are by nature compassionate and loving. These qualities are hidden in especially gifted individuals. A résumé will not give hint to a person's propensity of spirit, nor is it to be found in their outward demeanor. It rests in the heart. It is inherent in those who desire to assist old folks with their daily chores. Today these individuals are rare finds. In a world filled with superficialities there truly are individuals who want their lives to be significant and serve a purpose greater than their own selves. I have often wondered how it happens that so remarkably few of us set ourselves apart from the mainstream and look for meaning in life and a purpose for living – brushing aside all the add-up-to-nothing trivia. One afternoon I chanced to see a group of young applicants being led on a tour; they were looking for jobs. They each held in hand a résumé. The guide would know already which individuals might be considered. Those who were trailing, ambling, scuffing along, lackadaisically looking at the ceilings could have stayed home. No amount of training could quicken their steps.

√ *The Second Prerequisite: The next of kin, often sons and daughters, should request a meeting with the resident nurse or his/her representative and with the administrative director or his/her representative. Scrutinize the kitchen and critically appraise the complimentary luncheon. Is this the refreshment especially commended in the brochure? (I have learned the menu is the gauge of corporate profit.) In every way you can think of, be certain that this future home for your loved one is competent to provide what is promised. Ask questions. Ask questions. Ask to see the State Health Department's report. Carefully read the resident contract. Ask questions. Ask questions.*

When we older folks move into an assisted living community, our former normal and comfortable routines are replaced with scheduled activities. This takes some getting used to. I am impressed with how few of us have a hobby that we can bring along, particularly handiwork, but then, those knitting instructions have become too complicated and the print too small. And, as well, these earlier talents were not pastimes but instead they were most practical occupations. We did not prepare ourselves to be idle. Hence these retirement communities offer and encourage participation in a variety of activities. Tactfully encourage your family member to enter into these pastimes, first perhaps through merely watching others' enjoyment and participation. It is acknowledged that mental and physical exercises are beneficial to one's general health and well-being, i.e. happiness.

√ *The Third Stipulation: Making sure your loved one is properly cared for is not relegated only to the assisted living staff. Dianne, our activities coordinator, told me that she is disheartened that so many families 'drop their parents off and that's the last that we hear from them'. She added, 'It's so sad.' (May I add that it is sad, unnecessarily sad, for both parties?)*

I sit next to Irma at supper. She just celebrated her hundredth birthday. Her daughter Judy is unwaveringly attentive to Irma's well-being. Last Easter she brought along her own two-year-old granddaughter decked out in a very cute bumblebee outfit – striped yellow and black leotard, stockings and gossamer wings, and Irma became a little girl again. It is a little thing? No, it is a big thing.

√ *The Fourth Awareness: When you come to visit your loved ones and enter their world, leave yours outside. Turn off your cell phones and put away your electronic gadgets and click games. Speak slowly and clearly as you would speak to a child. Older folks do not hear as fast as they used to.*

Be inventive. Bring along a photo of the grandson attending college in faraway Utah; or perhaps an assortment of oriental teas or a comfortable snuggly sweater.

√ *The Fifth Consideration: If, for any reason, you cannot come for a visit, drop a note in the mail. When the mail is delivered, we oldsters take special care that we do not throw away a personal correspondence hidden among cleverly camouflaged junk mail advertising patio doors and seamless gutters. Commercial cards say nice things but a written word is very meaningful, heartfelt.*

√ *The Sixth Insight: We old folks are set in our ways. We are sometimes childlike but we are no longer malleable. If we have always had our breakfast at 6:30 and now the tray comes to our room at 7:47, we must get in touch with our children; they will calm us down and explain (again) that this turn of events is not all that bad; many people have to get along without any breakfast at all. They might even suggest that while we are waiting we will have time to say a morning prayer for the easing of others' greater pain and suffering.*

√ *The Seventh Awakening: This has to do with our understanding of what is happening as we get older. Aunt Martha, sitting quiet and alone, is gradually losing her connection to this world. Her system is fatigued after being twisted and bent by the winds of circumstance and time. Many years ago she was jumping and dancing, and years ago she was working and providing, and not so long ago she was looking back and remembering. Those years served her purpose. They comprise her journey. Now this phase of her life is approaching its end. It is not a sad time, for inside she is well and whole. We must not let outward appearances distract us. (A few days ago Ada celebrated her one hundredth birthday. I congratulated her and, smiling, she looked up and said, 'I feel sixteen.')*

Today, it is very easy to become so attached to the material world that we cannot recognize the deeper significance of what we are looking at. The attributes and qualities that identify dear Aunt Martha truly are Aunt Martha; they comprise all that we can know of her. Her materiality (the afore-mentioned atoms and molecules) merely enabled her personality to be known. Her attributes are deathless; her physical composition is merely the means whereby these attributes are brought out into the open and when this loved one's physical or mental constitution weakens and has advanced to the degree that she can no longer communicate, perhaps is not even able to acknowledge our presence, we sit with her quietly, silently avowing our affection. Bothering her to respond to and participate in inconsequential conversation is not relevant. Aunt Martha is moving. Her old house is no longer her home. She is all packed up and, if we observe carefully, we will understand that she has already crossed the bridge and comes back to be with us only fleetingly and on occasion. Her friends and family look on, mystified with her acquiescence. We hardly know what to say. We do not need to say anything. Aunt Martha is teaching us. Let us be attentive.

*

Well now, having said all that, what is it really like 'living in a place like this'? Well, some of us are very content and some others are complaining about everything – we love it – it's our art form. We don't want to hear about it yet we truly are set in our ways. But, after all, these are the ways that brought us to where we are. When we enroll in this finishing school, we do not doff our customary costumes to reveal ourselves in fresh and comely attire. It is too late to put on airs. Rather, we bring with us who we are.

This is good. Real people are presents, all wrapped up differently.

An assisted living community is perhaps rarely a sanctuary set apart from the outside world; some of these residences stand up better than others. Each one necessarily is a sampling, a thumbnail sketch of the world's larger picture. (In our later years surely we have learned that the perfect haven we seek is not of this world.) This is why we must be cautious; an assisted care facility is a business enterprise that relies on profit. That said, when we become residents, much of what we leave behind will be happily dispensed with – happily because all those former concerns resolve to things of little current value;

their importance gradually disappears. Adjusting one's personal routine to comply with the care community's schedule becomes, in fact, most comforting. Scheduled mealtimes and activities provide a framework which will accommodate nicely our former structured mode of living.

And this is good. Finally, we'll get organized.

Having someone nearby, someone who is always available when there is a need is most assuring. Dispensing our medications in a timely manner becomes the responsibility of the nursing staff. Heather, Head of Nursing, is most competent. As is Charley, in Maintenance. If the water closet keeps running, or the faucet drips, tell Sylvia at the front desk; she is the grand expediter. She will put you on Charley's 'next list'. Need to go to the grocery store for a bottle of shampoo or a battery for your hearing aid? How about the bank or post office? Do you have a doctor's appointment? Sandy, the bus driver, will get you there in a jiffy. In the final analysis, we have not lost our power; actually *we are more significant than ever*! All these people are waiting on our call. Without us, they would have nothing to do.

So far, so good! Now we will have more time for important things, like getting acquainted with new friends – and, actually, this is quite easy.

Listening to others makes them feel good. This is a wonderful way to gather people around us. We can learn much from their stories and ideas. Listening to what they have to say will endear them to us. This is not a ploy, a maneuver to garner new friends. Rather, listening furthers our education. With each and every story there comes a fresh approach to understanding. Behind the simplest of tales are significant meanings. Ninety-six-year-old Lovey told us that, when she was a little girl living in southern Alabama, she '. . . *ran, I mean* **I ran***, three miles to school. The one-room school house had two doors, even though there were only nine of us in there. School lasted only three months – in the summertime. After school I would run, I mean* **I would run** *back home – back over the bridge and back home. At night, I mean every night, I could hear "them" big old alligators down by the river; I listened to them moan. I mean they would m-m-o-o-a-n-n!'*

And Pauline: *'When I was seven years old and living in Cincinnati, Ohio, I too ran from my house up the street to school. Every morning I had to be very careful, watch my step to avoid the thundering herd of wild-eyed cattle racing towards me, being driven down the main street to the slaughter house.'*

And Morris: *'I'm a Turkish Jew; the only one you'll ever meet!'*

Morris and John and I shared breakfast together. Morris was a quiet chap, rarely venturing to share his thoughts; not so with John and me. We had opposing views on, say, whether the atom is alive or dead. John favored the second proposition. As we elaborately expounded our theories, Morris attentively ate his oatmeal. Exuberantly hovering around the intriguing difference between the meanings of sight and insight, I asked John if he thought that the Chinese character symbol for 'sight' might be enhanced to signify 'insight' with a mere flick of the inked brush. Morris, seemingly sharing the insight with his oatmeal, whispered, *'The Chinese have other problems.'*

Monday evening after supper our Conversation Club holds its weekly meeting. We tell stories and, well, '. . . ΩΕ ΤΑΔΚ ΑΒΟΥΤ ΕÇΕΡΨΤΗΙΝΓ ΕΞCΕΠΤ ΕΑΧΗ ΟΤΗΕΡ.' To start us off, the program might pose a throwaway question: 'Have you always been younger than your parents?' Or later: 'Do you think that competition in the schools might lead young boys to become aggressive and even violent in their later man years, perhaps resulting in wars?'

Julie joined us for her first meeting and, sitting quietly, ventured to say, *'I'm just going to listen. I don't have any stories.'*

Touching lightly on this and that, the conversation continued to the closing hour and then Julie, her eyes seemingly focusing nowhere, spoke: *'My father was killed in a coal mine accident.'* This caught our attention; even those who had nodded off woke up. She told how it had happened.

'When I was little, I grew up in southern Kentucky. We lived in a small house on a little plot of land, both owned by the mining company. My father worked in the big underground mine. The mine owners gave my father permission to use the coal from the outcropping behind our house so we could cook and have heat. One winter morning my father took my brother, who was 12 – four years older than me – back to the hill to get some coal. It was really a mountainside. His pick axe broke into a seam and the rock and coal fell on him. He pushed my brother out of the way just in time to save his life.'

The Conversation Club was speechless.

*

So, there you have it. All and all, do I recommend such a place as this? I do, but we must be assertive and mindful. And, who am I? Look out there on the porch . . . over there; the old fellow in the rocker, waving at the cars. Yup, that's me.

And don't just drive by. Come on in. We'll have a cup of coffee together. I'll tell you some stories. I've got some good ones.

*

Part Two

The Myth of Mortality

I believe I was a typical wondering child. Looking back, viewing my life from the outside, the whole scenario appeared as a narrative, the plot unfolding without my bidding. Yet I know that even little incidents, like my life, comprise the whole of history because everything is connected and, this being so, nothing is without significance. Big things rely on little things. Alongside these outward feelings, inside there were questions stirring. Who is this small wondering person and where is his place in this chain of events? I recall tales about children of an earlier time who were told, 'Don't ask so many questions! Go out and play!' but this isn't my story. Whenever there was a free Saturday or holiday, my family would set out for the museum or aquarium or planetarium, there to hear tell the lessons of life. And we were not alone. These learning centers were packed with people hungry for knowledge of the workings of life. Little children were entranced.

I cannot fathom why I should find myself at home in this engaging environment; it is a precious gift. As a guileless youngster, why did I, perhaps inordinately, muse over the mystifying behavior of Mother Nature and her fascinating family? Questions, questions. How can the ungainly caterpillar, while encased in a chrysalis of its own design and substance, in a matter of minutes, completely transform to become a graceful butterfly? How did the locusts learn to build a bridge with their own bodies so that the swarm could cross the stream? *How and why do things behave?*

I believe my own private excitement was a sampling of the larger world's coming of age. Child-minds, like mine, were responding to the motivation of the most prodigious transforming period in all of human history. After the incubation of countless relatively repetitious epochs and eras, mankind was entering a world that was previously unknowable. Ordinary people were discovering new ideas and hidden truths as their minds became fertile soil for new growth and great expectations. Our grandparents, many of whom were engaged in agrarian pursuits, were to beget children who would experience the world in an entirely different light, and then their children would become researchers and technicians in fields that would have been for them, as well, incomprehensible. There was something miraculous happening, truly. Like the caterpillar, mankind was leaving behind forever an archaic insular existence. It would appear that bearing witness to this remarkable historical benefaction might be reserved, justifiably, for a special people. Could it be that you and I are samplings of such a chosen people? Why were we not born a thousand years ago in some remote archetypical setting? Embodying their genes, in what way are we now challenged to respond?

This opening of the floodgate of knowledge brought answers to many questions about the mechanistic workings of life. Science was to have a field day probing, dissecting and scrutinizing everything. But this expansion of knowledge also gave rise to ever more baffling questions, questions which are unanswerable still. For example: Our technical skills are well honed; through research and through knowledge gained we know that we human beings and all other life forms, minerals included,[1] are made up of like ingredients, atoms drawn from a warehouse of some 118 elements – oxygen, hydrogen, carbon, iron, etc., but this knowledge does not tell us what *causes these atoms to gather and align to form a stone, a plant, an animal or a human being.* Although the microscope does not reveal their essential character, atoms prove themselves to be living because they have an alliance with life, yet, as well, they are passive, not having a will to adapt to a rock's cohesive discipline or a plant's growing needs or an animal's senescent nature. And when these dispassionate bits of matter are engaged in human enterprises, they unwittingly serve to express ideas and to weigh options and to arrive at conclusions. They enable thinking but, of course, they do not think. They are the minute carriers of life, passing from one aspect to another.

Energy, the atom's single defining factor, does not respond when approached with practical tools of inquiry. The microscope reveals nothing of its nature. Nevertheless it is the lifeblood of the terrestrial world; in varying degrees its pulse is found in every created form called upon to reflect a presence. The mineral is lamentably demeaned when we deny it life, for energy must be no less at home in the mountain or stream as in the buttercup or giant redwood, in the gnat or hippopotamus or in us. In the ascent of consciousness from mineral to man, life cannot miraculously appear at some juncture where it is truly absent and then is truly found.

Sir James Jeans, the eminent scientist of the late 1900s, questioned and wrote:

> . . . is a living cell merely a group of ordinary atoms arranged in some non-ordinary way, or is it something more? Is it merely atoms, or is it atoms plus life? . . . We do not know the answer. When it comes it will give us some indication whether other worlds in space are inhabited like ours, and so must have the greatest influence on our interpretation of the meaning of life – it may well produce a greater revolution of thought than Galileo's astronomy or Darwin's biology.[2]

Sir James's insightful question is now answerable. Ascribing life to the atom will accord with what might be named the Era of Discernment, the time wherein common knowledge will inevitably lead to deeper understanding. When we cross this threshold and accept the oneness of Existence, acknowledging that *life's energy is inherent in the display of all phenomena*, we will understand that life needs physical matter only to display its presence; we will distinguish the reality from its phantom image. It will become common knowledge that 'every atom in the universe possesses or reflects all the virtues of life . . .'[3]

Thus it would appear timely that science re-examine its findings and name what it is that is *orchestrating* these atoms to behave and serve a purpose. It must be a label that does not carry a bias. Perhaps 'Energy' with a capital E to designate its supremacy would suffice. To the present time this has been a most disquieting dilemma, principally because behavior is not analytical, a something that holds still as we look at it, then to assign it a befitting category. So the question stands: What is the identity of the phenomenon that is manipulating will-less matter to serve its own agenda? This is not only an intriguing question but an important one; important because its implication broadens our perspective concerning the nature of life and the meaning of a personal existence. It is made clear: living things necessarily age but do they die? Can life stop? This is a most intriguing question. Do minerals, plants, animals and human beings use Energy to their advantage or does Energy use these forms to serve its purpose?

It is here proposed that the first proposition is flawed principally because physical matter – that is, atoms, molecules and cells – are passive, incapable of an influential initiative.

Be that as it may, today everything that is observable can be placed in its appropriate physical category, classified either as a mineral, plant, animal or human being. These various life samplings are universally acknowledged. We know the intricacies of what they do, but, as noted, we do not know what *causes them to do what they do.* This is still unexplored territory. Whatever this cause might be, it proves its existence in that we – you and I – can ask about it.

However, this we truly know: life is single. A deeper probe will reveal its countless applications. For example: the way things are (physically) constructed is determined by how they are obligated to (spiritually) behave. The following premise is interesting, particularly because it was discovered hidden in the disciplines of practical thought. The aesthetic credo stipulates that any form must yield to its function. It is a weighty premise. In the late 1900s the American architectural giant Louis Sullivan uncovered it and made it famous when he wrote:

24

It is the pervading law of all things organic and inorganic, of all things physical and metaphysical, of all things human and all things superhuman, of all true manifestations of the head, of the heart, of the soul, that the life is recognizable in its expression, that form ever follows function. This is the law.[4]

Louis Sullivan's insightful meditation reflects the expansion of understanding in our time. The startling dictum certifies that all physical compositions – mineral, plant, animal and human – are structured to be compatible with their surroundings, that is, to be in harmony with the ordered spectrum of life. And this implies that a particular physical form, *not self-willed*, is determined by the performance needed to satisfy a specific life function. Each of the four categories is made up of many individuals, a seeming mélange reflecting an endless diversity of color, form and behavior through a formula that cannot be accounted for, accordant attributes which are obviously not self-chosen. It becomes clear that Life's particularities are being used to facilitate an intent that is unfathomable. It follows that if we human beings *freely elect* to conform to this greater order, we are true to our purpose. As conforming is a non-physical process, a condition of behavior, it prompts us to concede that all the motivations that are sustaining the physical world are non-physical.

Indeed, another question that wrinkles our practical brow is related to this matter of behavior. It rests in the mystifying process of aging: being born, getting older and then, well, for some few of us, really old. We know how we enter this world, that is, through the loving alliance of our parents, we come into being, *we happen*; a genetic heritage is given a venue and longevity. If their particles did not meet, they would live only a few hours or days and the potential individual, composed very much like you or very much like me, would turn up missing.

However, hidden in this formative beginning there abides its inevitable end. Gerontologists study the aging process and through observation and analysis they come up with theories about why we get old. Some are convinced that the process can be tinkered with, even mitigated to delay aging's effects. People in eras past lived relatively short lives: in the 1600s, 30 to 40 was the average life span, whereas today it is somewhere around 71. (If you are 35 and a half years old, you are middle aged.) In light of today's developing technology, some experts claim to foresee that there is already born an individual who will live to be 150. This would be interesting. If we all were so immune to illness, eventually there wouldn't be elbow room to raise the kerchief to stifle a sneeze – but then, of course, there would be no need.

Be that as it may, throughout our lifetimes, wherever and however human beings thrive, we learn to sustain our physical and mental well-being through disciplining our appetites; that is, by carefully selecting appropriate nourishment and carefully weighing food for thought.

But our composition has its own agenda. It is in a constant state of transition as we vainly watch it evolve from one day to the next. Our constituent atoms, molecules and cells, enabling us to sense things, to see, taste, hear, touch and smell, are constantly being replaced as we stand by and watch ourselves get old – to the present, a somewhat wearisome, often clumsy, prospective.[5]

When we were little we were fed pureed carrots and now we enjoy them uncooked as in a salad. But carrot atoms/molecules are indifferent. They are like grist for our corporeal mill, passively filling the void left by their vanguards and, as we move on from infant to child to adult, ever more carrot atoms (or their like) are needed to sustain our advance – *until* we reach the point where our forging ahead is finished and we begin to retreat. As each of us withdraws differently, it would seem there is a personal tipping point where our crest is reached and we begin to slide downward. It is Life's puzzle. The whole process is achieved through the instrumentation of vibrant atoms which, having no materiality whatsoever and possessing no will to command or foresee, all the while serving us only briefly and without loss, persistently tweak us: *'What's getting older?'*

Setting out to discover the answer can be a most rewarding experience but it is necessary that we leave behind the conclusions of the past. We will start with a clean slate. Our summations are best sketched in; being newborn, they glimmer rather than blaze their truth. Logic will be our tool of discovery and the findings will be self-evident.

To start, we must acknowledge that Life is an all-inclusive system. In any of its constituent subordinate systems, like you or me, Energy is continually being introduced and dismissed as we grow and mature. This basic infrastructure is passive in its involvement; it cannot direct its own performance; and, as its surroundings are constantly in the state of motion, showing normal advancement in the response and behavior of *evolving cycles*, small cycles intertwining with ever larger ones, the replacement atoms, molecules and cells comprising this structure cannot instill their unalterable energy into a system that has completed its cycle. Any organization is made up of its components, again a system designed to operate in a pre-determined frame-of-function that does not accommodate evolvement beyond imposed limits. Charging such a framework to respond to a greater task is futile. Each cycle has a beginning and an ending but, because life advances, each fresh subsequent cycle is an enhancement of the one preceding.

Thus every living system exists by way of its cycle, and each distinct sequence is woven into the fabric of life. Moving on with this premise, it might be interesting, even important, to dissect this universal cycle-phenomenon and see how it works, perhaps then to see how we work, that is, how we experience our cycle, evolving from the point of our arrival to the instant of our departure – *if* we actually depart . . .

So, let's see. If we expand the theory, *everything is a consequence*. If we can accept this premise, we might then be swayed to place everything observable as the end-product of an ever-earlier initiative clearly taking even the two of us back to some sort of primal beginning. Would this not mean that we are necessary consequences of a directive that is inscrutable but commands universally? Certainly we ourselves and all these other effects surrounding us are not setting our own agendas.

A simple example. Your finger, striking the table, results as a tap. The sound exists but in its fixed state it can have no inkling of its cause, that is, the identity of your finger. And your finger is not privy to the constitution of your brain, the instrument that facilitated the exercise or, even more, an awareness of the mind, the brain's unknowable mover and master; and whence the mind? It is obvious. All these consequences exist but their *origination*, the essence of the cause that brings them forth, is hidden. Jotting all this down, the summation is predictable: all these after-effects, including the two of us, cannot embrace the make-up of the initiative that brings them forth; the motivation clearly is of a different province.

Granted, any effect is brought into existence by its cause but the cause needs an intermediary between itself and its effect. The *spiritual* initiative, the mind, requires a *material* link, the brain, to manifest thought. It follows that, for a potentiality, that is, for something hidden to become known, an intelligible instrument is needed for its representation. The virtuoso composes the concerto but he needs the violin for the music to become existent and his artfulness to be acknowledged. Otherwise his claim is vain. In like manner, the Supreme Cause[6] needs human consciousness that this hidden presence might be known. The instruments – violin and man – are physical but their potentialities are not. The violin without the virtuoso is just an intricate wooden box. It is when he puts the bow to the strings that he puts himself in his instrument and music comes into being. Likewise, the human instrument without consciousness is just an apparatus, a mechanism. It is when the Creative Will puts intent into the human apparatus that human spiritual attributes appear. It is a universal principle: mind + brain = thought; violinist + violin = music; Supreme Will + man = consciousness. Without the *material* intermediary, that is to say, the middle factor, the *spiritual* initiative would remain unknown.

History's grander picture records the ultimate underlying influence of this intermediate capacity in the linkage and servitude of religion's principles, the foundation on which civilizations are built, for *'They give spiritual life and are shining with the light of realities and meanings'.*[7] The myriad lesser cycles are mere instrumentalities enabling spiritual attributes to be progressively manifested in passive matter (be it mineral, plant, animal or human), then to be acknowledged as meaningful solely through human intellect. This ordinance warrants impassioned reflection. Briefly, without human consciousness, the world's repetitious cycles would be the end-product ultimately serving no purpose. 'Intelligence' is prescribed and mandatory.

Fair-minded scientists and religionists will find their accord in the recognition of the oneness of Existence, for the will-less matter confronting them emits Energy to become apparent only through the instruments of *sentience*, that is, the *physical* exercise of looking, touching, hearing, etc., then to be processed and regarded through human *consciousness* as having meaning through the employment of *insight*, that is, *spiritually* seeing, feeling and listening, etc. The accord rests in all materiality's dissolving to pure Energy (each atomically formed earthling is an energized structure whose inner properties are tagged nucleus, electrons, protons, neutrons, quarks, etc.) and Energy itself being 'outwardly' utilized to serve the universal Purpose. This most remarkable scenario is all-inclusive, be it in evidence in the physical world as a wildflower in the oxygen it provides or in the immaterial world, as in the Buddha's counsel through which hidden wisdom is revealed,[8] for the oneness of Existence necessitates that the material and spiritual aspects of life be governed absolutely similarly.

The potter is a good example. Using *only his will*, he shapes the dust of the universe to be a bowl. He puts himself in his creation; the shape of the vessel and the color of glaze identify him. The finished masterpiece is the *physical* effect of the potter's *spiritual* capacity to create. His earthenware cannot know from whence it came; and, as well, the base clay is the effect of a cause residing apart from and beyond its composition, for its earthen particles are not infused with a will enabling them to bond naturally then to become clay. Excepting for the degree of creativity, it is arguable that there is not a great difference between the potter (pure Energy) willing his pot out of nothing and the 'Creator' (pure Energy) willing creation out of nothing. So that we might discuss the phenomenon of life – the state of being – and death – the perceived state of not being – in this discussion we have adopted 'Energy' as this spiritual causal factor. In this particular instance it will serve as a substitute for 'Spirit', separating it from its customary religious setting. We will think of Energy as a symbol-word. As such, it will be the unknowable factor but it will be easily acknowledged as existent because energy, even as an accepted practical word, is still unexplainable. We have been searching for reasonable evidence of a 'Creator' and the understandable nature of Existence for a very long time. In the future, looking back, our milepost will mark the era where the rational thought of the scientist and the spiritual insight of the moralist first met and merged.

That Existence is single is not a hidden truth, but the branching out of this truth is truly mind-boggling. That every part of Existence reflects its heredity, its parent make-up, is fascinating, even mystifying. Analogies are helpful. Contemplating a large chunk of cheese, or the make-up of Existence, the tiniest crumb, a molecule bit, will have the same qualities as the whole; the properties of the stellar galaxies are not different from the properties of the atom. That matters beyond understanding, to the present, have necessarily been relegated to a spiritual province becomes the dilemma because 'spiritual' carries an exclusively religious connotation, whereas such favoritism is excluded from the condition of oneness. Our vocabularies are insufficient to serve our present-day intellects. We have too few words to describe the proven but still unknowable immaterial factor. Words such as physical, or solid, liquid and gaseous are specific. However, to acknowledge the character of the initiative that brings forth these effects, that is, what *causes something to be solid or liquid*, we must rely on words such as supernatural or paranormal or 'spiritual', and these words are quite inadequate. Our present vocabularies lack words that specifically define life's non-physical 'single state of being'.

It is fascinating that the cause–effect scenario has its foundation in the oneness of 'Existence'. It begins with the union of the primary Causal Factor (the initiative we have named 'Creator') and its consummate effect (named 'His' creation). They are so closely bonded they are as one. As Existence is single, not allowing duality, it is made clear that only the Creative Cause exists; the effects are contingent and provisional. They are emanations. *In the beginning was the Word, and the Word was with God, and the Word was God* (John 1:1). There is no duality implied. The fundamental oneness is initiated and thereafter manifested in the transposition of subordinate capacities wherein any effect instantly becomes the impetus of a new cause, each of which branches out to expand the oneness. The eminent scholar J. E. Esslemont[9] wrote:

> With every advance in science the oneness of the universe and the interdependence of its parts has become more clearly evident. The astronomer's domain is inseparably bound up with physicist's, and the physicist's with the chemist's, the chemist's with the biologist's, the biologist's with the psychologist's, and so on. Every new discovery in one field of research throws new light on other fields. Just as physical science has shown that every particle of matter in the universe attracts

and influences every other particle, no matter how minute or how distant, so psychical science is finding that every soul in the universe affects and influences every other soul.[10]

However, inherent in this oneness of things is the supremacy of the cause over its effect; in every instance the cause is initiatory, the effect is the consequence. It is obvious the effect is subordinate to its cause yet vital in its own servant state, for the initiative derives its identity only through its result, much like the potter *willing* his pottery to validate his creativity and mirror his image: *So God created man in his own image, in the image of God created he him . . .* (Genesis 1:27). Without you and me and the, at present, other seven billion human 'effects' worldwide, the reality of the Supreme Initiative would exist but the conception would not. Does this mean that Existence exists but becomes apparent only through our perception of it? Are we – you and I – that significant? The answer has to be 'yes'.

Weighing all these arguments, they add up to something like this: Life presents itself through the agency of cycles; cycles exist only through the interplay of causes and their effects; within each cycle the cause is incomprehensible to its effect but most important is the disclosure that cycles do not merely repeat, they advance through the process of aging.

The above discussion may seem remote from the theme of this essay, that is, exploring the processes of life with a new and pleasing outlook, but it is part of the summary that will lead to the understanding that life is single and positive; that every aspect of its behavior is necessary to its function – even aging, the phenomenon that allows life to evolve.

Exploring the proposition that life appears in matter in the manner of cycles is indeed interesting. However, this is not a new finding. Such concepts were discovered decades ago but they were mostly bits of knowledge, not brought together in a unified field as parts of a great oneness. The cycle of being born and growing old is now acknowledged as an inclusive process not designed only for plants, animals and people. The world itself is considered an 'organized system' that has a life span, and throughout its cycle plants and animals and people are formed from its base material. But there is something most strange that is happening within all these cycles. As any form ages and declines, it is also being renewed. In the mineral realm, over long periods of time, the oceans continually vaporize to rise up into the heavens, there to reform and return to wash the mountain into the valley, at the same time the mountain is being thrust upward.[11] At its very tip, fossil impressions of ancient sea creatures are laid bare. The mountains are dissolved while being reconstituted; were it not for this recycling of Energy the land would be lifeless and level with the sea. The plant springs forth from the seed and in the span of a cyclic season grows with great vigor; it can break apart concrete. In its span, as its strength diminishes, renewed Energy is transferred to the forming ovules, tiny pods of the same Energy that fueled the parent cycle. As the plant's life wanes, its offspring are invigorated to maintain and enhance the evolution. In the animal realm, the development of the horse from conception to foal to adult, and the evolution of the horse within the species, from the 11-inch-high *Eohippus* ('dawn horse', 52,000,000 years ago), to the 35-inch-high *Merychippus* (20,000,000 years ago), to the 60-inch-high thoroughbred of today reflects the dual relevancy of this cyclic law where participating forms decline while their heredities advance. We as individuals change and evolve from a fertilized egg held in our mother's womb to an awakening child to mature human being in just a matter of minutes (37,000,000, more or less). As our Energy diminishes, our children's and grandchildren's is strengthened. They are running, jumping and dancing, as we did with the same ageless borrowed genes. And the same metamorphosis is taking place in our kingdom as we, eons ago, evolved through the same process from perhaps a simple (but complex) Archaeozoic organic conglomeration, to perhaps a fish-like design, to the comely shape embodying us today. Our realm and we, held in the pristine substance of our respective wombs, have evolved together throughout our particular life cycles. The world (and the universe) and all its structures are living and dying simultaneously through the circulation of the universal Energy.[12] Much like the synchronal interchange of living and 'dying' cellular components in the structures of sentient beings, an underlying cadence is at work in all systems. Suffice to say aging is a mystifying business. It appears to come very close to being a spiritual matter, a proposition that is true but not explainable. That life manifests itself with organization and not through random happenstance might well lead us to seek out this synchrony and regulate our lives to comply with its self-evident mandate. I believe it is proven: life is defined by so-called spiritual attributes and nothing else; its singleness appears in the physical world merely costumed differently.

Spiritual matters in this context are more than wispy otherworldly traits; they break away from the age-old images of harps and clouds and idyllic pastures. Rather, truly, they are 'worldly' traits, definable and specific, yet elusive. For example: the soil's spiritual attribute is called *cohesion*, the affinity that bonds one atomic particle to another to affect a structure. Cohesion does not have physical properties that hold still as we look at them but they do exist. And the plant's defining attribute is named *growth*; its physical composition evolves demonstrably. The animal embraces these lesser attributes but its structure enables *sense perception* and *instinctual behavior*; qualities inexplicable but certainly present and accounted for. And lastly, *our* composition allows *rational thought* and *free will*, contemplative capacities that are not vague, rather they make our configuration of atoms 'human'. All these spiritual attributes are the 'substance' of the physical world, for without them the world would not exist; albeit without the physical

34

world they, of themselves, too, would remain hidden. When we remind ourselves that life relies on *bits of indestructible Energy* to serve its purpose, it is proven that, all in all, only life exists.

It is most interesting to note that in the human realm the linkage between the 'physical' and the 'spiritual' is facilitated with such practicality. Our materiality, composed entirely of passive lack-of-will particles, is so exquisitely aligned that our non-physical free will and our capacity to reason are authorized and are made available and are easily accessed by way of our physical tools of inquiry. As was stated earlier, eyes, ears, noses, tongues and fingers tie us to the material world but we *willfully redirect them to connect to the spiritual world* where the eye looks but *we see*, the ear hears but *we listen*, the nose smells but *we discern*, tongue tastes but *we savor*, the finger touches but *we feel*. Miraculously, our physical tools open the way to the mystical world of insight where knowledge crosses the bridge to understanding. Reassessing where the true substance of life lies, we will understand that the spiritual side of life reigns supreme over the atomic structures that bring it forth. And we will understand that the *'we'* part of the scenario is, as well, unequivocally and totally non-physical.[13] It becomes irrefutable: in this phase of our life's journey, spiritual attributes are adorned in befitting earthly attire that we might experience the meaningful lessons of life.

We ask, 'Meaningful in what way?' The answer surrounds us. Studying any living system, using the forest pond as an example: every species and kind is free to function in its prescribed cycle, yet is limited by innate constraints. Each form fits into the greater order without even a slight hint of dysfunction. In this micro-universe each of life's expressions, be it turtle[14] or waterlily, is meaningful in finding its place in the single state of diversity, the forest pond's spiritual mandate. In like manner, we become meaningful when we discipline our diversity to comply with this universal certitude. This universal overseeing authority is named 'religion', albeit 'juris-diction' or 'rule' may be more appropriate, as the obligation of response is implied; or perhaps 'faith', where surety and reliance underlie the law.

*

It is here that I must branch out from our theme and, as Esslemont recommended, examine a contingent truth. However, it is not a significant departure, as you will see.

'Religion' is one of those earlier-mentioned words that no longer serve us well. It is restrictive and has become threadbare and defenseless. To the present time religion's discipline has been construed to be relevant only to human spirituality but it is brought into this discussion because, in its pure unadorned form, it is not exclusive to human affairs. Rather it is central to the galvanizing of all of life's systems; it gathers the universal diversity to a single Purpose; it 'rules'. Religion's mandate is: to gain something more, there must be the giving of something less, in the manner of sacrifice, and this is relevant not only to human achievement: the dawn yields to the day; the seedling gives way to the flower; the caterpillar's landlocked attributes are surrendered to the winged flight of the butterfly. And, through man's renunciation of the essential worth of a solely material existence, knowledge of things is replaced with the understanding of things. Through this universal transformation, in observing its wave and wake, we are taught to break the bindings of our own physical restraints that we might soar in the realm of life's already existent immortality, there to reach our highest point.[15] We learn to 'leave behind', surrender all the burdens that tied us to the material world, thereby enabling the effect of a spiritual gain. Without this covenant, the obligation of surrendering the lesser state (material) to achieve the greater (spiritual), we would not advance, rather to remain fixed in a repetitious earthly revolving, as was earlier noted. Outwardly religion has served its rallying purpose, notwithstanding that at the present time we are chopping its oneness into doctrinal pieces and this fragmentation has resulted in universal chaos. It is made clear: the oneness of Existence requires that its two aspects be not only attending but also commensurate, even comparable. As there is but one physical sun that bestows life to the physical world, there can be but one spiritual bestowal that awakens all life to achieve 'spiritual' Purpose and perfection. Religion, without being tampered with, enables all life's systems to realize a greater bestowal through the sacrifice of a lesser one. For example, the mineral's dormant condition is reborn in the vitality of the plant; the plant's capacities are saved and elevated in the animal, and the animal's characteristics are made greater when subdued and enhanced by human attributes. This food-chain progression requires the absolute absorption of one state into the other; not a semblance of its former condition remains. Man's religion necessarily exists as a proclamation relative to his capacity of comprehension, his uncovering the hidden meaning of things, as there is no higher material condition to serve him. (We remind ourselves that none of these states is corporal; that is, the mineral's cohesion, the plant's attribute of growth, the animal's sense perception and human cognizance are not tangible.) Religion, by this definition, has been contemplated by man seeking knowledge of his place in the scheme of things since the dawning of intellect.[16] Interestingly, each succeeding outpouring reflects the phenomenon of the cycle. In its evolvement each has its start with the proclamation of its Founder[17] wherewith the universal Energy is planted in the heart of the tribe, then the clan and then the nation, the overall guidance facilitating man's synchrony with the evolvement of life's ever greater universal cycle. Each pronouncement grows with great vigor until it reaches its 'tipping point', where its vitality starts to fade and its cycle comes to a close. But history records that it is religion's fundamental jurisdiction that is the *cause* enabling man to adjust his behavior to comply with the evolution of this greater order, even though the initiative itself is incomprehensible. (The aforementioned tap, in its fixed state, might relegate *its* cause to a like province.) In essence, there is one jurisdiction monitoring everything; necessarily it is disclosed progressively, the subsequent outpouring fulfilling the endowment of the prior, the entirety being the motivation responsible for life's expression. This aggrandizement (the achievement of a higher state) in the 'lesser' kingdoms is automatic; their transformations are natural. The soil's attributes (cohesion, etc.) are enhanced with those of the plant (growth, metabolism, etc.) without consent; the plant's qualities are heightened when combined with those of the animal (sense perception, instinct, etc.). But mankind's metamorphosis requires willful intent.

The writings of 'Abdu'l-Bahá[18] are most helpful in understanding that life actually is governed by one universal law, that every distinct component is part of a great singleness which is eternal. He states: *'Nature is that condition, that reality, which in appearance consists in life and death or, in other words, in the composition and decomposition of things.'*[19] *'. . . the breath of life appears in plants, in animals and in men.'*[20]

These excerpts of 'Abdu'l-Bahá's writings command particular attention. In His statement it is made clear that 'the breath of life' is set apart from the forms that it uses. His use of the word 'appearance' is significant because it helps us understand that *it is the specific composition of matter, the alignment of its particles, that enables life to appear*, that is, to be manifested with particularity through matter's 'substance'. (The afore-mentioned Louis Sullivan 'discovered' this law decades later.) Many of 'Abdu'l-Bahá's discourses explicitly define life as ever-existent; what we construe to be death is merely a transfiguration of material composition. We must interpret the proposal thus: Life is ever existent and separate from the forms that it uses; however, it is unknowable until it is revealed in the shape and substance of matter. It becomes apparent – it appears in the form of 'beings'. As our earth's family of beings constantly taps into life's flow, each generation is necessarily enhanced to accommodate the prescribed evolution. As stated, life is not divisible, a portion assigned to the turtle and a greater allotment to the human. Rather, the turtle, or the human, because of predetermined accountability, embodies, yet constrains, the wholeness of life's presence. Its essence is ever intact, inviolate as the various physical systems unwittingly profit by its wholeness to their subordinate and designated degrees. Then life naturally, spontaneously, *appears* as attributes which we designate as mineral, plant, animal and human behavior.

But 'Abdu'l-Bahá's elucidation should not be so difficult a proposition. It is complementary, an addenda to what we *know* is true, i.e. that human beings are more than clever bits of random matter dancing with one another, constantly changing partners. Before science gained authority, religion was the dominant force in our lives; it ensured we towed the line with its dual promise of rewards and punishments. It would appear that religion has not kept pace by reconstituting its articles of faith with expanded meanings to accompany science's escalating knowledge of things to the end that our two aspects, the 'material' and 'spiritual', might provide a balanced environment in which we could grow, rather than the lopsided one to which we now so diligently attend – in a sense, looking for the meaning of life through the microscope's lens. But wait! True religion (not the man-made doctrinal one), in its pure untampered-with estate, does not lag behind. It is actually the impetus behind science's revolution wherein, *for the scientist, the moment of blossoming is often immediate, the 'ah ha moment', while the full bloom of the spiritual harvest takes longer, for it must slowly germinate in the soil of the human heart and grow.* Scientific discovery, the awakening of intellect (in the search of truth), in the context of the oneness of things, is itself, in its sudden ascendancy, the means serving to break down the barriers of empty superstitions and vacant religious dogma. This is 'Abdu'l-Bahá's assertion: *everything derives its purpose through a spiritual transformation.* Even His explanations are evidence of the blossoming of the expanded vision of reality that would not have been appropriate to an earlier time. They are truths *that now increasingly infiltrate the evolvement of all thought and learning, and thus ultimately are the cause of the awakening of each of the sciences and the fruition of each of the creative arts; in total, the human product.* (Baking a cake, caring for orphaned children; whatever the *contributory talent* might be, *it is the creative art abiding only in the human condition.*) Religion, then, is not a belief but rather a conversion; the changing into a different state. The material world becomes a spiritual Eden as is promised.

What does this idyllic phrase mean? Does the world become a place of pastoral bliss? Studying the records of the past, our world, a miniscule sphere in the vastness of the cosmos, has gone through its cycle marked by specific periods of maturation. We have tagged these eras Archaeozoic, Proterozoic, Mesozoic and Cenozoic incorporating numerous sub-periods and epochs, such as Cambrian and Jurassic or Paleocene and Pliocene wherein the world's ecology was able to display varying and increasing degrees of life's Energy. The dust of the universe was summoned to constitute an environment, each stage submitting to the maturing process without will. In this illustrious process, the predestined Eden was germinating, hidden in the cataclysmic dawnings of deliverance. The primordial world was being reborn constantly. There was not yet the will that might cause dysfunction, for man was abiding his time in this womb until his living accommodations were readied. The diversity of life was constantly being refined, in preparation for the custodian's arrival. To this point there were no boundaries, for the world was a single place of habitation; minerals, plants and animals shared to their measure the wealth freely without gluttony or greed; each cycle reflecting the inner harmony. Therein man's developing needs for growth and survival were being met as he evolved in his own realm as with the others in theirs, all as parts of the great oneness. As his capacities of reason and intellect gradually emerged, man left behind what he perceived to be constraints to his freedom; breaking away, setting out on his own path in search of fulfillment. Discovering free will, he rejoiced with this new toy, manipulating the laws of nature; taking command, defying gravity as he flew through the air and sailed under the seas. It was then that the world's spiritual wealth was mistakenly perceived to have monetary value, and it was then that he divorced himself and reappeared to the environments surrounding him, not as husbandman but as usurper and profiteer, guilelessly using the world for his own gain, without expectation of reprisal. Mistakenly, in his arrangement with life, he thought the world was his for the *taking* rather than for the *borrowing*. When he discovered that he was living by happenstance atop a universal resource, he claimed ownership, to the deprivation of all others. Once used, he polluted the air he breathes and the water he drinks.[21] Self-satisfaction and greed set him apart and he is spiritually bankrupt and alone.

Thus, at the present, we find we are outcasts inflicting our dysfunction everywhere while our environments struggle with the neglect. There remains the hope that it is not too late to instrument the reverse of our behavior. The remedy is simple; but it has always been simple. We must view the material world as paradise, a silent partner in the achievement of our spiritual orientation. Then the world will become an Eden.

*

This whole scenario is an unprecedented disclosure. The two disciplines, science and religion, have always been contenders for authority but now, by way of 'Abdu'l-Bahá's elucidations, the oneness of their missions, i.e. the nourishing of the material and spiritual aspects of human nature, are effortlessly resolved. He addresses the apparent contention with profound clarity To paraphrase: *Physical matter is not physical and thus the laws monitoring its behavior reside, as well, in the non-physical realm.* That the behavior of matter (formulated as atoms, cells, molecules or organisms) is monitored by spiritual decree becomes irrefutable. Complex theories are swept away with the assignment and administration of an intent that is not generated within the matter being scrutinized. Science will continue to hover over the answer until the light of deeper understanding breaks through the mists of outward appearances. It is understandable that we are captivated by its wonders. The world has been transformed through its seeming magic; a seduction that has directly robbed religion of its wreaking of revenge on the sinner. There is too much majesty displayed in the organization of life, often viewed through the microscope's lens, for such a dire perspective to prevail. A grand awe is called up in its scented streams that beckons us to drown ourselves in its bounty. Our free will allows us to do this. Or, we can sit on the bank and watch it flow past – an ill-fated heedlessness. Worldwide, are we not being called upon?

'Abdu'l-Bahá's profound explanation of the workings of life makes clear the force that is monitoring everything. He speaks as an 'emissary' for the new cycle of mankind's spiritual evolution in that He is the exemplar of this latest Revelation,[22] the culmination of the greatest of all cycles knowable: *'Know of a certainty that in every Dispensation the light of Divine Revelation hath been vouchsafed unto men in direct proportion to their spiritual capacity.'*[23] Our capacities are now world-embracing, the cycles of the tribe, clan and nation are mere mileposts marking our former residences and the accompanying provincial leanings are unbecoming. It is self-evident: *'The earth is but one country, and mankind its citizens.'*[24]

The foregoing discussion is a necessary part of this thesis

as it makes unmistakable that *all aspects of the human condition are included in the oneness of Existence.* Diversity is humanity's foundation: if we all were identical and equal, the 'oneness of mankind' would be a meaningless phrase. Religion **unadorned** is mankind's only unifying catalyst; no other overseeing agency will ensure this harmony. This spiritual outpouring is always relevant to our capabilities, for we ourselves limit the bestowal. However, the avenues to true understanding are to be no longer sidetracked by vague interpretations. They will be paved with the creative arts and sciences of our liking. Humdrum will be replaced with enthusiasm for learning the verities of life, and under this canopy our diversity will find its single perfection, which then will mirror its perfect single Cause.

*

Now, returning to our theme, immortality. When the fuller manifestation of life is withdrawn from any of these sentient forms, we look on these circumstances as sickness or death. For example, when the turtle's Energy becomes restricted, lessened by irreversible illness or aging, we have deemed he is approaching his life cycle's end. As the ebbing escalates and turtle-behavior is no longer possible, his atoms begin to disassemble and the turtle is pronounced dead. But wait. Where did the turtle go? Did he just disappear into thin air? Where is the part of him that is now missing?

The following premise is satisfying because it is based on reasonable evidence. As stated, Existence is a system. Similar to cycles, large systems incorporate ever smaller systems and each one maintains its integrity through the interaction and compatibility of its components. For example, the system named 'forest pond' calls upon its constituents to represent and sustain its wholeness; the constituents have no say in the matter and cannot do otherwise. Energy is manifested in each distinct form so that the pond might function. When the individual constituents have completed their tours of duty, the system is not affected but continues in its perfect state through the constant recycling of its unalterable, indiminishable Energy, to be allocated and infused into subsequent forms. Deploying its bountiful vitality equitably, the pond's completeness is maintained. For a brief time the pond's Energy is partially particularized as a 'turtle', then again abides as neutral to be used endlessly in the pulse of his replacement or that of others in the pond's life systems. We choose to name this paddling, organized micro-system 'turtle' when it functions in a defined and exact manner through specific knowable turtle traits. When this behavior is withdrawn, it is no longer a turtle. The assortment of atoms, now merely resembling a turtle, gradually dissolve into other forms as its Energy is reassigned.

So where does the turtle go when he 'dies'? As any existence cannot become non-existent, it must be that this perfect particularity named turtle is returned to the perfect greater particularity named pond from whence it came, much like a drop of water is returned to the ocean, the components of the one being necessarily equivalent to the other. Not one of the pond's systems draws its make-up from an outside source.[25] And, as well, beyond question the turtle and his/her mate are, through their blended genetic attributes, living in their descendants where they will thereafter perpetually abide as each subsequent generation is energized to participate in life's ever greater evolutionary cycle. And our household pet, the one whose loyal affection was the return for our loving care, did he just disappear? Or does he live in the storehouse of our memory, itself an adjunct to our own immortality, *the only state wherewith every 'being' is credited with having existence.* Those of us who have experienced this loss are often consoled by an awareness of the pet's continued presence. Awareness of our own 'non-departure' will possibly be strengthened when we become intimately familiar with our own spiritual reality and its deathless habitat. This argument will sway us to its favor when we accept and apply the conclusion of science that reveals all compositions of matter – household pet included – to be composites of Energy having no materiality whatsoever.

And what about us; what is the manner of our 'death'? When we are conceived, the atoms that comprise our personal make-up are not new, nor are they randomly or freshly picked from the mineral warehouse with its 118 selections. Certainly deathless atoms, perhaps those that enabled some ancient terrestrial form's existence, now serve you and me. And certainly they or their like are the same reusable 'particles' that accommodated the genetic formula facilitating each of our own ancestors' life cycles . . . back into eternity. All forms then and now draw their existence from life's single, inexhaustible wellspring of Energy. If it is true that the gene pools of our ancestors are employed to facilitate our present life cycles, the question arises: what constitutes the motivation that utilizes these genetic attributes to further life's evolvement? They were expedient to the past. It is apparent that each newly-conceived human being is imbued with capacities commensurate with the prescribed evolution; that the 'new individual' is the means for progress; there is no other.

However, although each of us is defined by attributes that are human, our particular heritages, that is, the diverse gene pools of our dual ancestries, *give us personal specificity, personality*, and these spiritual qualities, once they becomes manifested, *abide forever* because, as discussed earlier, attributes, general or specific, are not *of* the material world, they are the *cause* of the material world. They are put to work 'manifesting things', using the materials at hand. When our physical cycle is completed the atoms that served us remain vital in other forms, leaving us, the essence that used them, vibrant and whole. Nothing *goes* anywhere!

When a loved one is away in a far distant town, our love is not

*diminished by her absence. If we are told that this loved one died
two weeks ago, why did we not at that time immediately feel the
loss? When the dreaded symbol-word 'death' is mentioned, why do
we react as though the event had just happened? 'Oh, I am so sad;
our loved one is no longer with us.' But she has not been with us
for two weeks; why the sudden bereavement? Certainly her attributes have not disappeared. We love her now no less than before.
We will miss her image but this was put aside 14 days ago while
we felt nothing of it. Is she 'confirmed dead' merely because we are
privy to the news?*

My dictionary describes life as *'the quality that distinguishes
living organisms from dead organisms and inanimate matter,
manifested in functions such as metabolism, growth, reproduc-
tion and response to stimuli'.* It is the *'interval between birth and
death'*. And death is described as *'the termination of life'*.[26] The
new vision will clarify and expand our understanding, and
these definitions will no longer be satisfying. They are mis-
leading, mainly because death describes non-life, and where
do we go to find such a condition?

A brief review of 'Abdu'l-Bahá's explanation will be helpful.
Physical matter is composed of living atoms – living, in that
they cannot be devitalized or put to death. Specific mineral
atoms are assigned to compose physical forms having no
prior existence. These forms are not randomly assembled;
rather, as stated earlier, their diverse configurations are fash-
ioned to channel particular behavior. The Supreme Cause[27]
delegates appropriate elemental particles to effect the oneness
of Existence. Minerals and their cohesion, plants and their
metabolism, animals with intuition and instinctual behavior,
and human beings with their cognizance, all serve as instruments to display the spectrum of life – to the end that life
expresses Purpose, that is, unity through diversity. On any
prepared planetary sphere, the progression from mineral to
human provides the necessary capacities to enable, as econom-
ically as is possible, this evolution. (Skipping from cohesion

to sense perception, without the metabolic state, would be impossible, as would Purpose being achieved without intellect.) It is interesting to note that at one time our own planet appeared to be lifeless and silent. However, this was an illusion, for the atoms within each constituent element – whether on Earth, Mars or far-away Eris – are dancing with life, abiding the time when they will be called upon to form a molecule or a cell, perhaps a flower or bird, or, eventually, a you and a me. Purpose enters the flow constantly, for the universe pulses Energy. *'Know thou that every fixed star hath its own planets, and every planet its own creatures, whose number no man can compute.'*[28]

So long as a natural and befitting configuration and balance is maintained within each structure, that structure will behave in a prescribed way. If circumstances from within or without intervene, or the normal longevity is attained, the structure and its chemistry will begin to change and the plant, animal or you and I will start to devitalize and, as we choose to say, 'die'. The curbing of life comes to all forms when their compositions are rendered inappropriate for particular and necessary degrees of Energy to be manifested. The mineral realm (atoms of Energy) is exempt from this summary as it is, in total, life's deathless enabler; it does not have a life span. Life as plant or animal or man is easily acknowledged and in these venues each cycle is made clear. Oftentimes, during the life of these sentient forms, Energy will be suppressed until the substance's integrity is reestablished – given water or nourishment, even a gentle touch. When this happens, Energy can again become appropriately displayed. We call this a 'recovery'. Actually it is the recovery of the capacity of the enabling substance to disclose the greater natural spiritual presence.

Energy could never depart; there is no place for it to go. Rather, the structured forms it uses are in a constant state of motion, coming into existence, serving Purpose, *and then they depart*. We human beings are ever existent because once our attributes are brought forth (through our atoms' service) they become a part of the eternal realm. It follows that we too do not 'go somewhere' when 'death' occurs. 'Abdu'l-Bahá says:

> Some think that the body is the substance and exists by itself, and that the spirit is accidental and depends upon the substance of the body, although, on the contrary, the rational soul is the substance, and the body depends upon it. If the accident – that is to say, the body – be destroyed, the substance, the spirit, remains.
>
> Second, the rational soul, meaning the human spirit, does not descend into the body – that is to say, it does not enter it, for descent and entrance are characteristics of bodies, and the rational soul is exempt from this. The spirit never entered this body, so in quitting it, it will not be in need of an abiding-place: no, the spirit is connected with the body, as this light is with this mirror. When the mirror is clear and perfect, the light of the lamp will be apparent in it, and when the mirror becomes covered with dust or breaks, the light will disappear.[29]

This singular explanation clarifies the vague interpretations of the past. Substance is relegated to the station of servitude; it is idle until called upon. If physical matter is the matrix that Energy uses for its own purpose, then it is without intrinsic value. When the plant or animal dies, having fulfilled the need of Purpose, its particles are recycled. The same atoms then behave as the mineral state allows, abiding – and Energy remains absolute, unaltered, unabated. Likewise, when our composition is no longer able to satisfy its assignment, it too is put aside. However, because of the specificity of the alignment of atoms that conjoin at our conception, particular deathless attributes are given a venue. Throughout our lifetime we can reflect personal and explicit human qualities which are eternal. As these distinctions define the center and core of our being, they are us and we are them. Thus we are everlastingly secure; we live on – unaffected by 'death'. To base our lives on this working principle, we must acknowledge that our spiritual attributes comprise our whole being. They are our essence. Our bodies are mere practical manifestations of Energy, subservient to its command. Humanity, then, is the common factor. Each of its individuals is marked with its identity but, as well, each is enlisted in giving human life diversity, our hallmark.

I believe that it is proved. Life, through all of its expressions – that is, by way of its various enabling forms (mineral, plant, animal and man) – is certified as single. As in the small forest pond where each of life's representatives is connected and contingent, it follows that *the reality of every possible composition pre-exists*; that is, spiritual attributes abide potentially. They are not exclusive to the material world; rather, on occasion, they are herein reflected when a particular capacity is called upon to maintain Earth's perfect state. Attributes are 'at home' here on this plane and in the realms beyond. Therefore, as man's essence is inherent in the eternal realm, which is not reliant on location, his relevance is befitting whether the province is composed as matter or is independent of such restriction. However, life's Energy becomes acknowledgeable continually in our worldly domain by way of our *non-physical consciousness*, the bridge whereby the evolution of the greater order is conveyed and made accessible to all life through this spiritual engagement. The entire evolvement being thereby channeled, the mineral, plant and animal capacities are merely stepping stones to the ascent. Were it not for man, the lifting up process would lead nowhere. Without man's spiritual capacities of reason and understanding being alerted, timely thoughts spoken and those scribed on new and ancient tablets would not exist. The capacities of the lower forms are unable to willfully respond. Nor are the convoluted folds of the physical human brain storehouses of inspiration to be meted out to accompany the evolution of Earth's ongoing cycle. As these effects, i.e. the appearance of progressive accumulated thought and initiative, enter our consciousness oftentimes unbidden, their source must be the wellspring of life's Energy that exists universally without location. It enters our practical world only through us by way of what we have named the Supreme Will, the Will of the Omnipotent Potter. We would be empty vessels otherwise, for any composition is unable to independently act.

It is made clear. The essence of all things, be they mineral, plant, animal or man, permanently abides in the spiritual realm, that is, every existing component's natural residence is in the unknowable province, whether it is hidden therein or manifested in the shape and substance of matter. If certain attributes are needed in this world, they are brought forth, but their residence does not change. The physical world, made up of atoms of Energy *and nothing more*, becomes the essential 'educational environment' where man learns to participate in the cycle of life's evolvement through his *willful* participation and compliance with the greater order. As was stated earlier, throughout preceding eons, before man's appearance, this classroom was being prepared for his attendance; will-less matter was being utilized and configured in preparation for mankind's edification. Without this material classroom (the universe), man's spiritual education is impossible, for free will needs an appropriate learning environment, the environment where the consequences of behavior are made explicit. All in all, Existence is his home. His presence is hidden until the dwelling-place is prepared.

Existence incorporates a method wherewith the wholeness of life is infused in all of its structures. Minerals, plants, animals and human beings are not arbitrarily assembled; rather the full bestowal of life is therein particularly refined and processed to facilitate the natural and greater evolution. In the ascent of life, from mineral to man, particular capacities inexplicitly merge. The mineral is absorbed by the plant without integral loss of its attribute cohesion; the plant is consumed by the animal while its capacities of growth and metabolism remain intact; the animal incorporates these 'lesser' attributes, augmenting them with sense perception and instinctual behavior, attributes which are unaltered when they are in the human condition. Over all, life's evolvement appears in the guise of a means whereby *all base matter* is directed to serve an ultimate Purpose, that is, to prepare and maintain the physical environment (the classroom) wherein, as stated, mankind can acquire his spiritual education. He brings with him *his own means for learning*, that is, his intellect and free will. Man's physical structure is so finely tuned that life in the human degree is able to appear therein naturally and, through his freedom to investigate phenomena, he is able – and is henceforth charged – to respond to the supreme injunction, the moral code incorporated in religion's fundamental edict, the law that assigns man the responsibility of willfully mirroring 'back' to their source, the entire spectrum of life's attributes, for he embodies them all. Then creation, through man's free will, reflects the perfection of its parent origin, the oneness of Existence is confirmed and the purpose of life is fulfilled. Inherent in the premise is our immortality. It is assured because the spiritual attributes that then serve to define us are designed to comply and merge with the evolving, ever-existent, non-material eternal order.

*

Before bringing this essay to a close, it would be a neglect not to acknowledge the influence of my parents' lives in this whole regard. I was introduced to these ideas through their interest in the Bahá'í teachings and these principles gradually became the backdrop for each of my life's episodes. When my father, Carl, was 24 years of age he traveled from Chicago to 'Akká in the Holy Land to visit 'Abdu'l-Bahá when He was still a prisoner. I remember him telling of the behavior of 'Abdu'l-Bahá' jailors who, when leaving His presence, would address

Him as 'Master' and bow their heads as they backed away. I
vaguely remember my mother singing contralto in duet with
Albert Windust at numerous Bahá'í functions. The cookies on
the refreshment table probably held my greater attention but
gradually I absorbed the Bahá'í principles and, as a youngster,
never thought of these concepts as 'religious', as they are more
universal in scope. They connected me to the world of nature,
the out-of-doors, outside the doors of the isolated environments of synagogue, mosque or church, rather to the harmony
of the ponds and streams of the forest glen. Harms Woods, a
short bicycle ride's distance from my home, was my spiritual
childhood retreat. Here I would watch the frogs and turtles
and the myriad darting wiggly things, not realizing fully that I
had entered a spiritual domain. The oneness of life surrounded
me and embraced me as I experienced a powerful affinity with
this natural setting. Accordingly, they became a corollary to
the Bahá'í principles. The concept that life is governed by one
universal law, that every distinct 'thing' is a part of a great
oneness, pressed me to investigate these teachings more thor-
oughly. Hence the concept that religion is a constant, every
moment, personal comradeship, not to be called upon on
occasion, has accompanied me wherever my path has led and
whatever my circumstances have been. I could find no dis-
crepancy between science and religion, particularly because of
the one principle that positions the material and the spiritual
under the same canopy; the one that examines the physical
structure of the material world and its accompanying spiritual
performance, the one that explains the oneness of life and its
immunity to death. This principle enabled me to see the need
for diversity, then to view, *without discrimination*, the sanctity
of each participant and its incumbency. The concept is simple
but abstruse. According to the Bahá'í philosophy, Existence
is a single state but its evidence has aspects. For instance,
'Heaven' is the state of perfection and 'Hell' that of imperfec-
tion; the one is harmony with Purpose, and the other is the

want of such harmony. Thus, just one condition exists; it finds its identity only when it is measured by its various 'aspects'. Our children might invent a simple game: What is smooth? Smooth is something that is not rough but the something is single, for the opposite of something is nothing. A bottle can be full or empty, a person can be learned or ignorant, a door open or closed, but the principle factor exists in its own single state. It has no opposite identity: a bottle's opposite is a non-bottle, an inconceivable proposition. Thus every existing 'thing' is single, a state that is invulnerable; it is not altered by any influence. If it exists, it exists in its singleness. It is like Truth. There is one Truth which is the state of absolute perfection. If something is untrue, like a lie, it is merely the absence of Truth; it is a vacancy. Similarly, there is only light; dark is merely its lack. At night the sun still shines. Therefore life is the single positive state of being and death is simply a symbol-word used to give life acknowledgment and identity. There can be no 'non-life'. Only life exists.

So, where do we reside when our material cycle ends? This excerpt from the Bahá'í writings consolidates the promise of all past ages.

Know thou of a truth that the soul, after its separation from the body, will continue to progress until it attaineth the presence of God, in a state and condition which neither the revolution of ages and centuries, nor the changes and chances of this world, can alter. It will endure as long as the Kingdom of God, His sovereignty, His dominion and power will endure. It will manifest the signs of God and His attributes, and will reveal His loving kindness and bounty. The movement of My Pen is stilled when it attempteth to befittingly describe the loftiness and glory of so exalted a station. The honor with which the Hand of Mercy will invest the soul is such as no tongue can adequately reveal, nor any other earthly agency describe. Blessed is the soul which, at the hour of its separation from the body, is sanctified from the vain imaginings of the peoples of the world. Such a soul liveth and moveth in accordance with the Will of its Creator, and entereth the all-highest Paradise . . . The nature of the soul after death can never be described, nor is it meet and permissible to reveal its whole character to the eyes of men. The Prophets and Messengers of God have been sent down for the sole purpose of guiding mankind to the straight Path of Truth. The purpose underlying Their revelation hath been to educate all men, that they may, at the hour of death, ascend, in the utmost purity and sanctity and with absolute detachment, to the throne of the Most High. The light which these souls radiate is responsible for the progress of the world and the advancement of its peoples. They are like unto leaven which leaveneth the world of being, and constitute the animating force through which the arts and wonders of the world are made manifest. Through them the clouds rain their bounty upon men, and the earth bringeth forth its fruits. All things must needs have a cause, a motive power, an animating principle. These souls and symbols of detachment have provided, and will continue to provide, the supreme moving impulse in the world of being. The world beyond is as different from this world as this world is different from that of the child while still in the womb of its mother.[30]

*

Overall these are breakaway disclosures, samplings of understanding, freed from the static interpretations of yesterday, untied from ancient religious dogma and practical worldly science, and this is the very reason contemporary minds, experimenting with pure logic, will see the light of certitude more clearly. This enlightenment is a natural consequence of the coming-of-age of human intellect; the overview is so broad as to encompass everything. Provincialisms are to be replaced with universality. Peace and harmony are to radiate from the single realm of Existence as all the constituents fit into the

greater order. The necessity of universal peace is not only relevant to human society but to human society's harmonious
relationship with all societies that make up Earth's ecology, to
the end that our world becomes 'a gem in the diadem of the
Universe'.

'Abdu'l-Bahá 1844–1921

Author's Note

This treatise is clearly unconventional but, as the process of aging is an ongoing study and death is still a mystery, an unorthodox approach – one that incorporates, by way of logical argument, the spiritual aspect of life, one even assuring that true death is an illusion – certainly would be germane to this theme. As I mentioned in the Introduction, these words and phrases are possibly inept. They cannot convey the depth of implied meanings as perhaps do the allusive words and phrases quoted above. This premise is not a pie-in-the-sky, dreamy yearning. It is a fresh approach to understanding the phenomenon of life and death and, if embraced, its practical line of reasoning undoubtedly will help us face the aging phenomenon and its aftermath with a happier outlook ☺.

HS

Bibliography

'Abdu'l-Bahá. *The Promulgation of Universal Peace*. Wilmette, IL: Bahá'í Publishing Trust, 1982.

— *Some Answered Questions*. Wilmette, IL: Bahá'í Publishing Trust, 1981.

— Tablet to Dr Forel. http://reference.bahai.org/en/t/ab/TAF/taf1.html.utf8?query=forel&action=highlight#

The American Heritage Dictionary. Boston: Houghton Mifflin Harcourt, 5th ed. 2011.

Ask a Naturalist. http://askanaturalist.com/dowereplaceourcellsevery7or10years/

Bahá'í Faith. www.bahai.org

Bahá'u'lláh. *Gleanings from the Writings of Bahá'u'lláh*. Wilmette, IL: Bahá'í Publishing Trust, 1983.

Dhammapada. Various editions.

Esslemont, John E. *Bahá'u'lláh and the New Era*. Wilmette, IL: Bahá'í Publishing Trust, 1980.

Great Pacific Garbage Patch. http://en.wikipedia.org/wiki/Great_Pacific_garbage_patch

The Holy Bible. Authorised King James Version. London: The Gideons International, 1957.

Jeans, Sir James. *The Mysterious Universe*. Cambridge: Cambridge University Press, 1930.

Shoghi Effendi. *The World Order of Bahá'u'lláh*. Wilmette, IL: Bahá'í Publishing Trust, 1991.

Sullivan, Louis. 'The Tall Office Building Artistically Considered', in *Lippincott's Magazine*, March 1896.

References

1. In the ascent of consciousness from mineral to plant to animal to man, the atom, the basic elemental component cannot be 'dead', say, in the mineral state and miraculously become alive in the growing plant.
2. Jeans, *Mysterious Universe*, pp. 6–7.
3. 'Abdu'l-Bahá, *Promulgation*, p. 286.
4. Sullivan, 'Tall Office Building Artistically Considered', in *Lippincott's Magazine*, March 1896.
5. Present research suggests our body cell structure, with some exceptions, is replaced over a period of some seven years. See, for example, http://askanaturalist.com/do-we-replace-our-cells-every-7-or-10-years/
6. In this essay, Primal Cause, Supreme Will, etc., are used to depict the unknowable nature and identity of what we pragmatically call Creator.
7. 'Abdu'l-Bahá, *Some Answered Questions*, p. 162.
8. For example: 'Victory breeds hatred, for the conquered is unhappy.' *Dhammapada*
9. Scottish physician, linguist, author.
10. Esslemont, *Bahá'u'lláh and the New Era*, p. 209.
11. See the work of James Hutton, 1726–97, Scottish physician, geologist.
12. Astronomers observe the simultaneous birth and 'death' of galactic systems.
13. The logic of the premise is fascinating: our being is human, one of being's four single states (mineral, vegetable, animal and human). This condition of being is diverse absolutely in its make-up; each individual, defined only by his/her spiritual attributes, comprises the whole spectrum of human diversity. Each individual adorns this being with particularity through the gene pools of ancestry. As these personal spiritual attributes are unconditionally immune to death, it is plausible we do not go anywhere when our material cycle is finished. The premise is: to us, the material world ceases . . . leaving us intact.
14. Note: this book uses the North American definition of 'turtle', meaning any member of the chelonian order.
15. In my part of the world this sacrifice is interpreted as mankind's 'salvation', i.e. being 'saved' from a meaningless, detached existence

('Hell'). The new perspective is relevant to all life forms' deliverance and rebirth.

16. It is an ancient argument. The premise here builds its foundation on the oneness of Existence: this eternal existent system embraces everything; all phenomenal potentialities for life's expression are inherent therein. Therefore, mankind has forever existed potentially, and when the appropriate physical environment is so constituted for his manifestation, he naturally appears. This means that man and his capacities are in the dust of the universe.

17. Historically, the moral teachings and social laws of Krishna, Zoroaster, Buddha, Moses, Christ and Muhammad; currently, those of the Báb and Bahá'u'lláh.

18. 1844–1921; eldest son of Bahá'u'lláh, the founder of the Bahá'í Faith. In His Tablet to Dr August Forel, 'Abdu'l-Bahá explains the living atom. See http://reference.bahai.org/en/t/ab/TAF/taf-1.html.utf8?query=forel &action=highlight#

19. 'Abdu'l-Bahá, *Some Answered Questions*, p. 3.

20. ibid. p. 73.

21. See, for example, the Great Pacific Garbage Patch, http://en.wikipedia. org/wiki/Great_Pacific_garbage_patch

22. See www.bahai.org. The premise is that religion is single, it is revealed progressively. The titles of its revealers, the Manifestations (Krishna, Buddha, Moses, etc.), are necessarily named with the alphabets of the time. Tens of millions of us have fought and died defending ethnic words having common meanings.

23. Bahá'u'lláh, *Gleanings*, p. 87.

24. ibid. p. 250.

25. The life system named 'pond' ascribes Energy, particularized as 'turtle', in the degree appropriate to maintain its equilibrium. The integrity of the system determines the number of turtles allowed.

26. *American Heritage Dictionary*, p. 489.

27. Jehovah, God, Allah, etc. are symbol-words. They serve to represent the single Primal Cause, the essential creative impetus of Existence, above and beyond terminology or nomenclature, certainly transcending personality.

28. Bahá'u'lláh, *Gleanings*, p. 163.

29. 'Abdu'l-Bahá, *Some Answered Questions*, p. 239.

30. Bahá'u'lláh, *Gleanings*, pp. 155–7.

Printed in the USA
CPSIA information can be obtained
at www.ICGtesting.com
JSHW080051200923
48724JS00002B/156